Solving the Retirement Puzzle – What you have, what you will need and how you will get there

Ian King, CFP^{CM} Professional & Chartered Financial Planner

Published by Ian King Financial Planning Ltd.

Solving the Retirement Puzzle – What you have, what you will need and how you will get there

01332 856 373
www.iankingfp.co.uk

Ian King Financial Planning Ltd is authorised and regulated by the Financial Conduct Authority (Firm Reference Number 630542). Registered in England & Wales 08469955. Registered Office: The Old Vicarage, Market Street, Castle Donington, Derbyshire DE74 2JB

ISBN: 978-0-9931731-1-0

Contents

Dedication

To all of my clients, past and present, who have challenged, encouraged, frustrated, inspired and most importantly trusted me.

Acknowledgements

This guide could not have been written without the support of my team. My thanks go to my assistant Gina Deacon for organising me, to Lucy Ludlam for helping me with the initial draft and to Eleanor Shean for help on the content and revising the manuscript.

I would also like to thank Emma-Jane Black whose wonderful designs and illustrations adorn this guide.

About the author

Seizing his passion for helping clients and their families achieve a brighter and more rewarding future, Ian founded Ian King Financial Planning in January 2015.

With over twelve years' of experience in advising clients, Ian is able to call upon a wealth of knowledge and experience in developing and delivering a wide range of client solutions. Ian's expertise ranges from legacy and estate planning, retirement planning and aiding those people who need assistance in paying fees for Long-Term Care (LTC).

Always seeking to improve both the service to his clients and his own professional development, Ian is proud to be a Fellow of the Personal Finance Society and a Chartered Financial Planner. He has also achieved the status of Certified Financial Planner[CM].

In order to help develop his skills further and give a much stronger service to his clients he also enjoys spending time with his team to help put processes in place and develop their skills and knowledge of the financial services industry.

Away from the office Ian's interests include travelling to new and wonderful places, language learning, trips to the movies and spending time with friends and family.

Ian King Financial Planning

Introduction

Why has this guide been written?

The main reason for writing this guide is that we believe people need a greater understanding of the concept of retirement and what it means to them. There have recently been significant legislative changes which impact upon how people are able to answer many questions, for example; how can I fund my retirement? What will retirement look like for me? And what will I need throughout my retirement?

Retirement matters are commonly the cornerstone of many individuals' financial planning needs and hence we want to help people make more informed decisions about what is such an important part of their lives. To do this we hope to use our expertise to bring clarity to those who read this guide and, hopefully, allow them to achieve the retirement to which they aspire.

Why it is important for people to think about retirement

There are lots of misconceptions about retirement and this includes some of the following areas:

- When people can retire
- What different plans they have
- How to save for retirement
- How to access their benefits at the start and throughout their retirement.

These misconceptions are created by many factors including both changes in legislation and society and it is important to clear up these misconceptions. What appears to be a very complex topic actually once you have cleared up the misconceptions can become quite simple. This guide aims to bring simplicity to people.

Some of the things we are concerned by are changes to society and how people are saving for their older age. Historically generations past have primarily done this through two ways. Firstly the State Pension which is a guaranteed income and starts for everyone at a certain time, currently age 65. Secondly through a company "gold plated" pension scheme.

People would often work for their whole career either for the same company or for the government and they would accrue what's called a defined benefits or final salary pension scheme. This means that they would get as a pension a certain proportion of their final salary when they retired. Often if you worked for a full 40 years that would mean you would get two thirds of your salary as a pension. This is how it used to be.

Looking at the options people have now, firstly the State Pension is going through changes which means that the longer term benefits from this are going to be more limited.

Generously funded employer schemes are now few and far between and certainly a great number of the defined benefit schemes that the previous generation and even the generation before benefited from are no longer around, unless it must be said you work in the public sector.

This means that we are now in many ways on our own as individuals to start saving for our retirements. Most people who are working will be or have already been made a member of a pension scheme through a government initiative called Auto Enrolment but those benefits are calculated in a different way to the schemes that the previous generations benefited from. These benefits are solely linked to the amount that gets invested into the scheme from the employee and the employer (known as a defined contribution plan). The contributions that go into such a scheme are more often than not limited relative to what previously went into employer pension schemes twenty to thirty years ago. So in effect the onus to make up that gap is on every individual and their family.

Unfortunately in my opinion no one has really stood up and said what this actually means. No politician has stood up and said it's uneconomic for the government and for employers to carry the burden as they did previously. They have shifted the burden onto the individual and what that means is we all need to personally save a lot more.

If we don't then we will have to retire later or at least work part time into our retirement or have less to live on in retirement than perhaps our parents or grandparents did. In effect this is a huge time bomb that people are not aware of; they are sleep walking into retirement nd they will be shocked when they come to retire to find out that the upboard is bare.

Quite simply more and more people will find that they don't have nough put away through their State Pension, private pension, mployer pension or other savings to make sure their money lives onger than they do.

It is important to look at this sooner rather than later. There is never time that is too early to look at this. The sooner you can get at least n initial understanding of what you have and what you are going to need the better.

The main problem is that people don't have much of an idea of what they already have and what they are entitled to from the State. The State Pension amount is changing and alongside that the age at which people can take their benefits. It used to be that women would get their State Pension at age sixty and men at age sixty-five, it is now currently age sixty-five for both genders but it is going up over time. Many people now in their twenties and thirties won't see their State Pension start until they are sixty-eight or even older.

Likewise they don't understand the raft of pension plans they have now as people commonly will work for a series of employers, frequently changing employer and when they leave they will be left with a little pension pot from that employment which will be very separate from their other provisions and may well have different types of benefits to which they have no idea how they all fit together. They may have also made some of their own provisions in a personal pension which then gets added into the mix alongside their employer schemes. There is a whole range of different benefits and that is something we are going to clarify in this guide.

Several steps were taken by the Government in 2006, these steps were meant to lead to pension simplification however they have only acted to make pensions more complicated as they bought in new rules but the old existing rules in many regards had to be kept. So in effect this created another layer of complexity for people to understand.

As a result of all this complexity allied to declining annuity rates mean that a lot of people are being forced or have been forced to take a lower income for the size of their pension pot than they would have previously.

ensions have now therefore become a bit of a 'dirty word' and as a result has led to people switching off from thinking about their retirement. The reality is that pensions are just one part of retirement planning; a pension is really just a way of funding retirement but it isn't the only way. We are trying to help people achieve their objectives which will not necessarily be done in the same way as their parents did or many other people they may know. This need to take a different approach is exacerbated as rules have changed again recently, and will likely to continue change in the future.

There has been much more liberalisation and how you can access funds from your existing pension schemes at retirement. In effect you can now take as much out of your pension scheme as you wish. That is subject to the pension scheme allowing you to do this. Some plans you may have now will allow you to utilise these new rules but some may not and of course it is important to work out whether you should use them in the first instance?

A lot of people and the press have spoken about people taking out their pension funds to buy a Lamborghini or some other similarly outlandish extravagance. That may be all very well and good but most people are going to want their pension funds to make sure they have enough income to live off for the rest of their lives. So it's really trying to make sure that you are protected in that regard rather than wanting to splurge all in one go and raid your pension plans.

The final reason we wanted to write this guide is because of all this complexity it is very difficult for people to simplify all the various different issues for people in an accessible and plain English manner and hopefully this is what we will achieve with this guide.

Who is this guide for?

The audience for this guide is primarily people who are still working and are yet to take their pension benefits, but they may be very close to doing so. Ideally also someone who may have been able to save something in various forms whether that's themselves and or through an employer scheme but is certainly looking to save further into the future between now and when they come to retire.

Commonly when we meet a lot of new clients they don't understand what they have got, so this is also a guide written for people who don't understand what they have already. Likewise many have no real concept of what they are going to need.

Some of the common questions about retirement we hear include:

- What is retirement going to look like?
- What level of income am I going to require in retirement?
- Is it going to be the same every year?
- Is it going to be slightly more in the early years in retirement?
- What are the impacts of long-term care?

This guide probably isn't for people who have large sums or capital, or need large sums of capital available to them or have particularly complicated needs. These sort of people would need specialist advice which a guide of this nature can't really cover. We can however help people in these sorts of situations but that's another guide for another time. This guide is really aimed at people who are unsure and are perhaps asking some of the following questions:

- Are they short?
- Do they need to save more?

People with those kind of questions in mind may also be asking:

- Can I retire early?
- What if I am forced to retire early? I.e. due to health issues.

What is retirement?

The first place to start is to discuss what retirement is seen as to most people. Frequently this would be considered in some ways rather like a line in some sand, whereby someone moves from full time work to no work at all immediately. You go to work as normal on a Friday morning and come teatime you have retired. Often that is at a set age, commonly the State Pension age, so many men look forward to their 65th birthday, it's their retirement. Or potentially it's an age defined in their pension plan which was set when you originally set the plan up as you are always required to nominate a date when the pension plan is set to run to. That doesn't mean you have to take the benefits at that date, or that you can't take them before or possibly afterwards.

That's often when people come to us and say we have these pension plans but I don't think that I can retire before a certain point in time.

Sometimes the answer is no, but again it's looking at this idea from more of a slightly different approach to what most would usually take. It's trying to look at pension plans as being separate from retirement. Pensions I repeat are only one way to help fund retirement. There are other ways and in fact Pensions can help achieve other objectives like providing for your children when you have passed on. There are many different options out there.

We try to use the concept of financial independence, rather than retirement being a certain date where I stop going to work.

Financial independence is the concept whereby it's the point at which you don't need to work for money ever again. This doesn't have to mean you stop work. You can keep on working it also doesn't mean you have reached a certain age. It does mean thereafter you have flexibility in what you do with your time and your income. You have greater control of your lifestyle. So what we do is work with our clients to help them achieve financial independence. How we do this will vary from person to person but we start by helping them understand what retirement would look like for them and what that would cost them.

1.   How Do Pensions Work?

is important to demystify ne types of pensions vailable. People frequently et statements from different ension schemes usually on n annual basis. If you are ke many people in their orties, fifties and early sixties ou may have three, four, ve, or six or even more ension plans.

ou will get statements that are ten to fifteen pages long for each nnual statement. They have lots of technical jargon in them and so many people just get them and file them away and never look at them because they don't understand what they mean.

We therefore need to get to grips with how different pension schemes really work. The simplest way to understand this is that there are, in the simplest sense, two types of pension scheme - one is a defined benefit plan which is a pension plan where your entitlement is based on an income per annum or per month and (should) provide a guaranteed income. The other type is a defined contribution plan and this is where your future pension benefits are dependent upon a fund value. We will look at each of these types of pension plan in turn:

Defined benefit pension plans

Usually a Defined Benefit Pension Plan is something that has been arranged by the government or your employer. What you would have done or are doing is paying in a certain amount of income or National Insurance Contributions (the State Pension is a defined benefit pension scheme). In return for your Contributions you will get the promise of a certain income in retirement. There will be a set date which those benefits will come into effect and if you were to take them before that point, if that's an option at all, you would have a reduction in your promised income.

Commonly your own contributions into the plan would be made out of your pre-tax income so in effect you save or you don't pay income tax upon the contributions. When you come to retire your pension income is taxable. A common misconception is that the State Pension is tax-free but that's not correct. The State Pension is taxable but in almost all cases it is paid before tax and your personal income tax allowance will cover any tax liability. What it does mean is that more tax will fall upon any other pension provisions that you have.

When looking at a company defined benefits scheme, this will also apply to say people who are members of the teachers', doctors' or police pensions etc. as they all have their own superannuation or defined benefit pension scheme. They all work slightly differently but there are some general concepts.

Whilst you are still working for the employer and are a member of the pension scheme you accrue years of membership. Normally that multiplies through to give you a pension equal to a set fraction of your salary each year. This is shown overleaf:

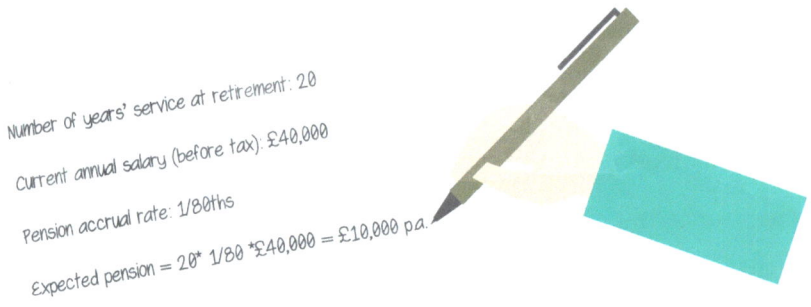

Number of years' service at retirement: 20

Current annual salary (before tax): £40,000

Pension accrual rate: 1/80ths

Expected pension = 20* 1/80 *£40,000 = £10,000 p.a.

If you are a member of an eightieth scheme that means you accrue one eightieth of your final salary for every year that you work or are a member of the pension scheme. So your benefits grow in two ways:

1. By continuing to work with the employer. So for example if someone works for forty years and is in an eightieth scheme they'll get 50% of their final salary. So every year as time goes by they'll accrue a greater fraction of their salary.
2. By achieving increases in your pensionable salary.

Different schemes measure your final salary in different ways; it could literally be your salary in the final year of you being a member of the scheme is the salary that your benefits are calculated with. It could be the average of your salary in your final three years of membership or it could be the highest salary in any of the previous en years of membership, adjusted for inflation. Quite simply when you come to retire that is all worked out for you depending on the scheme rules.

The scheme will know how long you have worked there and this will be multiplied by the factor and again by your salary at that time. This will be your pension you are entitled to at a certain given time. Many pension schemes have a retirement age of either sixty or sixty-five.

Whilst you are also a member you will probably have a lump sum death benefit, otherwise known as death in service which will be paid if you were to die before you retire. That is commonly a multiple of your salary; two, three or four times are quite common. There may also be a spousal pension and that would be a function of the pension you accrued at that point. Note that this is not the pension you would expect if you kept working until retirement but the pension you had achieved at that time.

Many people come to us and say how does this work if I leave employment or the scheme closes? So in the latter case you may work with the same company but they have closed their defined benefit final salary pension scheme. What effectively happens is your benefits are some ways locked at the date when you leave or the scheme is shut. So the amount of service you have accrued and your salary at that point is effectively capped, the pension at the point is increased each year broadly in line with some measure of inflation until the expected retirement date. This rate of increase varies from scheme to scheme and from member to member. Some schemes are very generous, some schemes less so.

One common thing to realise though is that you are not therefore getting any benefit of any further accruals; you are not getting any extra years or your salary increases above inflation. You are also losing your lump sum death benefits. Commonly at that point the sole entitlement if you die before retirement whilst in deferment would be a pension paid to a surviving spouse, with nothing available as a lump sum, a loss potentially of several hundred thousand pounds of life cover when compared to being an active member.

The question therefore is, is there any way of securing the older benefits or do they just get lost? The answer is yes they just get lost. If a scheme closes down but you stay within employment often the company may offer death in service through a new pension scheme. All companies are being required to provide pension schemes and some employer contributions may be made but many of the previous

enefits are unlikely to be matched. Certainly when you choose to
ave employment with a company then all life cover benefits will
nd and this is something that is commonly missed when people
ave.

o the next common question that people ask is how do I take my
enefits at retirement? So firstly the pension that you are entitled to
hen it comes into payment will have some form of indexation i.e. it
ill go up in line with inflation or earnings. Again this varies from
cheme to scheme.

you die in retirement a fraction of your pension, commonly a half,
ill be paid to any spouse. There is unlikely to be any lump sum
eath benefit - it will just be a promise of an income for life of your
pouse, which of course if you are single or your spouse dies before
ou has very little or no value at all. Even in these circumstances there
no lump sum that can be passed to children.

common decision that needs to be made at retirement with these
rpes of schemes is about taking a lump sum. Under pension
gislation everyone is entitled to take up to 25% of the combined
alue of their pension pot as a tax-free lump sum. It is a very
omplicated calculation for schemes of this type but to get a rough

idea you can work out the value of your pension benefits by multiplying the promised income by the factor of twenty. You are entitled to take a quarter of that as a lump sum. To take the lump sum you do however have to give up some of your pension income whereby as a result you get a reduced pension and a tax-free lump sum.

Why would I need to give up pension? Most schemes will just quote a pension income. So they would say your final salary when you retire was £20,000, you worked here for twenty years in an eightieth scheme so twenty eightieths is one quarter. One quarter of £20,000 is £5,000 a year. So they can pay you, from age sixty for arguments sake, £5,000 a year pension for every year that you live and that will go up every year in line with inflation. If you die in retirement your wife or husband will get half of that, so £2,500 a year. Again that will be index linked. When both of you have passed away the pension ends.

Or if say you are entitled to a lump sum up front when you retire, you could take that lump sum but to do that you will have to sacrifice some pension income. This varies and the calculations can be quite complicated as not all schemes force you to sacrifice lump sum in the same way. But in round numbers it may be the case that rather than having a £5,000 a year pension you have £4,000 a year pension, plus say a £25,000 tax-free lump sum. The options are therefore £5,000 a year income and no lump sum or £4,000 a year income and £25,000 tax-free lump sum.

Remember the pension is taxed as earned income in the year it's paid and the lump sum is tax-free and is paid as a one off. This can be left to anyone else if you were to die subsequently.

These decisions and options will be outlined to the member when they come to retire but not always when they are away from retirement and have received their annual pension benefits statement, but this is a standard option that you should look at.

You should also note that if you are a member of a government backed or arranged scheme, often referred to as a superannuation scheme, you will often have some lump sum in addition to the pension income quoted. For example the old Teachers' pension and a lot of other public sector service pensions have an eightieth pension scheme, so you accrue one eightieth of your final salary for every year that you are a member of the pension scheme. In addition to that you get three times your pension as a lump sum. That is often worth less than a quarter of the total value pot so therefore you can take more by reducing your pension. You get three times your pension in addition in some ways for free. The private sector tends to not have this and all lump sum benefits need to be funded by a reduction in pension income.

One thing that people need to consider is if you have an old final salary pension scheme and you are no longer a member of the scheme but are yet to retire what do you do with it? Well firstly you need to take advice as this is a very complicated area and certainly there are a lot of sharks out there who make money out of advising people to move out of these potentially very valuable schemes into alternative arrangements whereby they get paid large fees and commissions. So always take advice in regards to these schemes.

In effect you will likely have two options:

1. Keep the plan going. Your pension entitlement will just keep going up each year in line with inflation. Again this varies from scheme to scheme as some rates of increase are higher and better than others.

2. To transfer your entitlement. The pension provider will give you a transfer value; a lump sum to transfer to another pension. Note not to yourself, this is a sum of money that

must be paid to another pension scheme in exchange for the entitlement of a pension when you reach retirement age.

With transferring your entitlement there are various different advantages, including the potential for the fund to grow faster than the income might go up. If you were to die before you retire your family may get more than what you would get if you were to die with the final salary pension scheme (for example the death benefits could be a lump sum). There is also greater flexibility about who this could be paid to, rather than just a surviving spouse.

You may be able to take your pension benefits earlier without a penalty if it's in a money purchase pension scheme. This is also not tied to the employer; a lot of defined benefit pension schemes are underfunded and if an employer goes bust then the pension benefits may not be paid in their entirety, if at all.

So by transferring away you are removing that risk, but you need to put this against the likely risks which are the performance of your plan would not be guaranteed, it could be poor and there are costs associated with arranging the transfer and having the fees paid from your plan. You should also receive on-going advice about such a pension scheme and the charges associated with this can also be met through your plan, which could therefore limit the potential for growth. So advice really needs to be taken from a fully qualified pension transfer expert.

One type of defined benefit pension scheme that nearly everyone has is the State Pension. Before we move on to look at the other major type of pension plan let's look a little further at how the State Pension works and how it is changing.

The State Pension

A State Pension is a promise by the government that if you reach a certain age and you have been able to accrue sufficient National Insurance Contributions you are entitled to a State Pension. The State Pension is changing from 6th April 2016 and for people who are yet to reach their State Pension age by that point they will be receiving their benefits under new rules.

To put the new rules into context we need to talk about the various different options that people have been accruing benefits on to this point.

he basic State Pension is a flat rate scheme which is currently in 016/17 £119.30 per week. You accrue benefits in the State Pension y the payment of National Insurance via your wage packet or in ertain circumstance a credit in lieu of national insurance (e.g. if you re low paid or are staying at home to look after children).

he State Pension goes up in line with inflation or earnings or some ombination and this is announced every year in The Budget by the overnment.

reviously people have been able to accrue additional State Pension nd that has been done in various different ways. Originally this was ia the Graduated Pension Scheme which became the State Earnings elated Pension Scheme (SERPS) and then latterly the State Second ension (S2P). The State Second Pension is the current scheme that is force but that is being stopped from April 2016. Effectively all those hemes were ways by if you had earnings above or within a certain reshold you are able to accrue additional pension on top of your ate pension.

o receive this top-up you had to be "contracted in" to the top-up heme. You would be automatically contracted in however you may ave been subsequently "contracted out" by being a member of one of more types of pension scheme. Commonly you would be contracted out if you were a member of a defined benefit plan via your employer. In this instance the government would transfer part of your National Insurance contributions to your employer to help them meet the cost of providing you with your defined benefits. In return your scheme did have to meet a minimum standard of benefits for the government to do this.

Another way in which you could be contracted out would be through an Appropriate Personal Pension (APP). This would be a decision that you would make yourself, independent of your employer, whereby part of your national insurance contributions would be re-routed by the Government into a personal pension. This fund would in effect be very similar to the money purchase benefits which we will discuss shortly.

So in short, if you were contracted in to the state pension you would likely gain a top-up to your basic state pension or if you were contracted out you would accrue either final salary benefits from your employer or a separate pot of money via an APP.

From April 2016 this is being changed as now everyone will have a basic right to a new flat rate pension which will be no less than

£155.65 per week. No further accrual or contracting out under S2P will occur.

Not surprisingly however this isn't as simple as it seems, or indeed should be. To help guide you I will give you some examples:

If you were contracted in for your entire career you will get the greater of your previous entitlement under the old scheme (basic pension plus top-up) or the new flat rate. So, if your State Pension entitlement under the existing scheme with your top-up would have been £170 per week you will be paid £170 per week. If your entitlement would have been £130 per week you will get £155.65.

The complexity arises if you had spent part of your working life contracted out of SERPS or S2P. In effect the government will pro-rata reduce your state pension entitlement back to the existing state pension level in accordance with the proportion of your career during which you were contracted out. So, if you had spent your entire career contracted out you will get just the current basic pension (£119.30 per week in 2016/17). If you had spent half of your career contracted out, and the other half contracted in, you will get a pension which, as a minimum, will be somewhere near half way between £119.30 and £156.65 per week).

Sadly this calculation is not really something that you, or indeed an adviser can perform with any great accuracy so the best thing to do is to request a State Pension forecast. The best way to get a State Pension statement is to visit https://www.gov.uk/state-pension-statement and follow the on screen prompts.

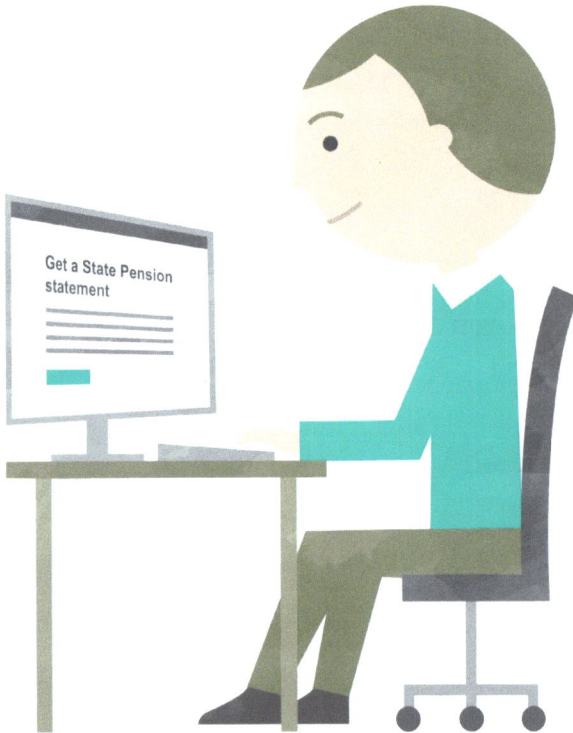

At the moment the government's systems are being updated so some people are getting projections under the new rules and some people under the old rules. Just take care when you get your projection to make sure you know which version of the rules that it is on. The bottom line will be those pensions will be projected in today's value so they will go up in line with inflation going forwards. Whatever hey quote on the projection should be a minimum; you can only get nore going forwards.

Defined contribution pension schemes

These types of pensions are whereby your pension benefits are dependent upon a fund value which is derived from how much money is paid into the scheme (either by you and/or your employer) and the future growth in the value of these funds up until you reach the point of taking your benefits.

Contributions will be made by you and possibly your employer. Often if it's an employer scheme they will match your contributions or put in a fixed percentage of your salary on your behalf and you decide how much that you wish to contribute yourself. As with defined benefit plans, contributions that you put in are made out of your gross income, so you don't pay income tax upon your monthly premiums. Your growth comes from fund performance, so you build up a pot just like a normal conventional savings pot. You put some money in and your employer puts some money in and the fund grows, hopefully, over time.

When you come to retire again you have options to consider including taking a lump sum which again is tax-free and is up to 25% of the fund. Fortunately in this case the calculations are much simpler, the entitlement is just 25% of the fund value. Then it comes to deciding what to do with the remaining balance – the 75%. In effect whatever you take out is taxed as earned income in the year in which you take it out. Commonly here there is two options:

Option one is an annuity which is whereby you exchange the pension pot for a secure income that is normally payable for life. There are various different options within an annuity that you choose at the outset. These could include whether you want to have the income to continue for a spouse if you die before they do and how and when you wish to receive your income. Some questions you may ask yourself when looking at taking an annuity are:

- Do I want the income to go up every year?
- Do I want to guarantee the income payments for a certain period of time, even if I die during that period?
- Do I want to make provision for my spouse?

These options are all chosen at the outset and once set up your income is free from investment risk. So the advantage of an annuity the known security of the income. It doesn't matter how long you ve the income will continue to be paid. The main negative of nnuities are that they are not very flexible - you cannot go back and hange your options in the future.

you are struggling with the concept one other way to look at an nnuity is to think of an annuity as a reverse life insurance policy. his is why annuities are provided by life insurance companies, they re selling the same product. With a life insurance policy you pay a nown fixed amount every month (the premium) for as long as you ve on the basis you get a lump sum when you die. You exchange a gular expenditure on your behalf in return for a lump sum when ou die. An annuity is the exact opposite, you exchange a lump sum hile you are alive for an income that's payable until you die.

he second option to taking a retirement income is through what's mmonly known as Income Drawdown, which is now extremely exible. In effect you have a pension fund which is similar to a giant okie jar which you can put your hand in and take out as much oney as you need. Whatever you take out, ignoring your lump sum x-free element, you pay tax on in that year. Effectively you decide ow much income to take and how and when to pay your tax. There re risks here of course and the main one is that the pension pot could be exhausted while you still need the money. You also take investment risk with the fund, the fund value can go down as well as up. So with a Drawdown plan the main question here is:

"I can take out as much as I want but am I taking a risk that there is no more income for me in the future?"

It's not necessarily as black and white as taking it all out in one go, it could be that you take a lot out in the first 5-10 years of retirement and then nothing later on. If fund performance isn't good for example then maybe the amount you can take out after that is limited. That may be ok for some individuals as you may decide that in the early years of retirement you are fit and healthy, there are things you want to do, let's enjoy life. You will sacrifice having a more limited lifestyle in retirement after that.

Crucially you will really need to make an informed decision if you wish to go down this route. Just taking the pension fund "willy nilly" and leaving the cupboard bare for your latter years without realising it is a very dangerous strategy.

One other advantage of this approach is it allows you to be more flexible with who you leave your money to. So if you are in the ortunate position that the pension fund doesn't run out - who gets what is left? You have more options with death benefits in drawdown han you do with an annuity and we will be discussing these later on n this guide.

2. Working Out What You Have

With this my approach would be – go into the box, the carrier bag, the briefcase etc. that has all your policy documents in. Take them all out and then open the envelopes and start sorting them out into piles. One pile for each individual policy you have. Every policy will have a reference number on it which will be unique to you. Sometimes this can be your National Insurance (NI) Number. Collect them into piles and then once you have all your piles of every individual policy put those piles into two separate sections.

One pile will be for all those benefits that are defined benefits so they talk about a certain income at a certain point in time. That will also include your State Pension. The other pile will talk about a fund value so they are defined contribution plans such as personal pensions etc.

Employer & Insurance Company plans

An old employer scheme will have the name of the employer somewhere on the documentation that is sent to you. It may be on the top in the form of a logo or it may have the logo of an insurance company on the document but with reference to the company in the header. As standard it will be on the first page of the statement that is sent to you. Your benefits here could be a deferred final salary pension which is going up each year in line with a certain amount of revaluation. It could be a defined contribution scheme which shows a fund value.

These types of plan could either be done directly through the company (i.e. they have their own scheme) and that's whereby you would have the name of the company in bold on top of the document or it could be with a life company so it could be referred to as a group pension scheme. Common life companies that operate these types of schemes include Royal London, Aviva, Legal & General, Standard Life and Friends Life for example but there are many more. Plans that are with these companies are likely to be money purchase pension schemes rather than defined benefit schemes. If this is the case they should be in the money purchase pension category of the documents you may have.

Moving on you may have personal pension schemes so these are the schemes that you set up yourself. Almost exclusively your benefits here will depend upon a fund value. There are some older schemes that have guarantees and we will talk about these in a moment but most of them are solely based upon the value of the fund. These types of schemes will be anything that uses words like personal pension, stakeholder pension, Self-Invested Personal Pension (SIPP),

xecutive Pension Plan (EPP) or Small Self-Administered Scheme
SAS). These will go into the money purchase pension pile.

he main exception to the rule that personally funded plans will go
ito the money purchase pension pile will be if you have a Retirement
nnuity Contract (RAC). These plans were the forerunners to
ersonal pensions and the main benefits are based upon a guaranteed
ension at retirement and hence these plans should be added to the
efined benefit pile of schemes.

heck for guarantees

o many old personal schemes have various different benefits and
ou really need to take advice and care when analysing these
chemes. Some of these benefits may include guarantees that could
e of great value, but others less so. It really depends upon the
idividual schemes but also your circumstances and how about
nportant they could be to you.

xamples of guarantees would be a guaranteed annuity, in effect
iaking your money purchase pension plan like a defined benefit
cheme and guaranteeing you a certain amount of income from the
cheme from a certain date in the future.

You could have a guaranteed annuity rate which is a rate that you are guaranteed to be able take from your available pension fund. Often these will be much higher than what you would be able to get in the open market now if you were to arrange an annuity. So for example it's not uncommon to have a guaranteed annuity rate of, say, 8% which would mean that you could exchange your pension pot of £100,000 for a £8,000 a year pension income, which will be much greater than what you would likely get in the open market.

However the questions that need to be asked in these situations would be:

- Do I need an annuity or maybe guaranteed fund values?
- Do I need to take my benefits at a certain point in time or in a certain manner to be able to benefit from the guarantee(s)?
- Is this worth much to me?

There could also be guaranteed bonus rates or performance on your investment funds. Commonly that will be the case if you are invested in a With-Profits fund. With-Profits funds are funds that are designed to invest in a range of different assets; stocks and shares, bonds, cash and commercial property. The With-Profit fund tries to smooth out the performance of the fund year to year with the use of regular and inal bonuses. The bonus they give you every year once announced cannot be taken away irrespective of the future fund performance. They can have a guaranteed bonus rate every year and often that could be higher than what is available in the open market.

Once you reach retirement age, or if you transfer your plan beforehand, they may provide you with a final, or terminal bonus. This however is discretionary and is designed to ensure that when added to your annual bonuses that you have received a fair return from the fund whilst you have been invested.

Moving away from With-Profits funds there could also be guaranteed death benefits, you may have additional life cover or you may be entitled to a lump sum when you die that is worth more than the fund as it is now. This could be a valuable benefit. Likewise and finally you may be entitled to a guaranteed lump sum at retirement that is worth more than 25% of the value of the fund. Again if you were to change that scheme you may lose that entitlement and it could be potentially valuable because that lump sum will be tax-free.

Bringing it all together

So here the approach to take is once you have collected all your pension information, is to make a list of all the benefits in those two different categories. You can then arrange your benefits in the following ways:

On the defined benefits side you start with:

- I'm entitled to a State Pension of £££ starting from my State Pension Age of sixty-five (for instance).
- I have a final salary pension scheme with XXX company that will pay me a pension income of £££ a year from age sixty for example.

Then look at your defined contribution schemes and add up all the fund values, please note that when you do this your fund values are not a promise of what you will definitely have at retirement. This may look like:

- I have £££ invested in an ABC personal pension
- A £££ defined contribution pension scheme with an old employer

- I have £££ in a stakeholder with XYZ insurance company.

Add all those values up and that will give you a good snap shot of what you have at this point in time.

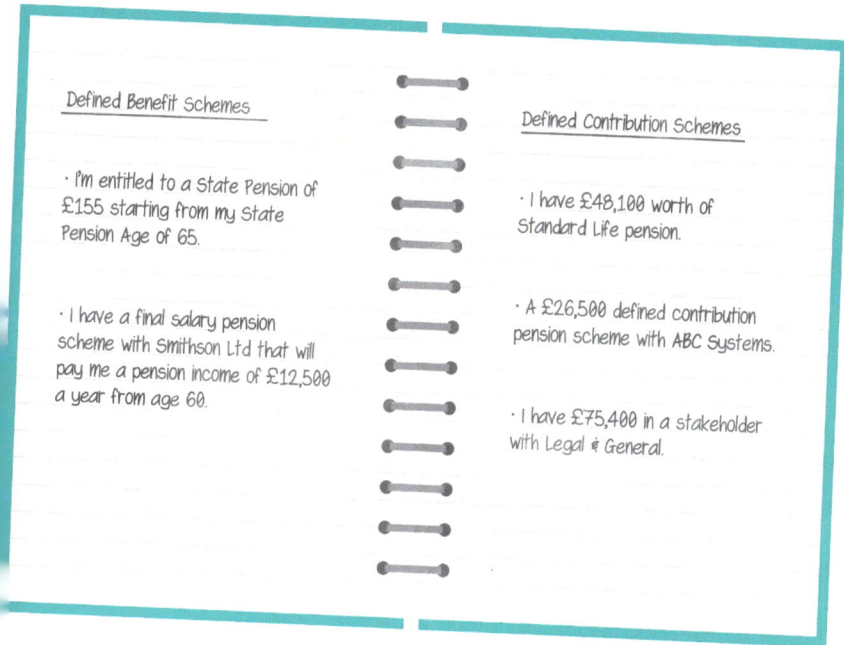

Defined Benefit Schemes

· I'm entitled to a State Pension of £155 starting from my State Pension Age of 65.

· I have a final salary pension scheme with Smithson Ltd that will pay me a pension income of £12,500 a year from age 60.

Defined Contribution Schemes

· I have £48,100 worth of Standard Life pension.

· A £26,500 defined contribution pension scheme with ABC Systems.

· I have £75,400 in a stakeholder with Legal & General.

When can I access my private pension benefits?

At present the earliest date at which you can access your pension benefits is your fifty-fifth birthday. Some schemes, particularly defined benefit schemes, may however reduce the income paid to you if you were to retire prior to your Normal Retirement Date (NRD), so particular care is needed when considering taking such benefits earlier than previously expected.

The government have proposed to raise the earliest age at which an individual can take their private pension savings from fifty-five to fifty-seven in 2028, the point which the State Pension age increases to sixty-seven. From then on the minimum pension age will rise in line with the State Pension age so that it is always ten years below. This change will cover all pension schemes which qualify for tax relief, with no exceptions.

3. What you will need

We use a document called The Budget Extender to help us get a greater understanding of our clients' income and expenditure needs and this we recommend you complete to start the process of understanding what you will need in retirement. A copy of the Budget Extender is available on our website, www.iankingfp.co.uk.

The Budget Extender will help you to list all of your incomings and outgoings. It examines income, expenditures, financial commitments, and discretionary outgoings both currently and a projection for retirement for you and your partner. The Budget Extender also helps to compare anticipated situations should either of you pre-decease the other.

You start off by looking at your current income from various different sources. So your earned income, investment income, rental income and you put all this down at the top of the Budget Extender.

Then you need to analyse all your current expenditures and here we think it's a good idea to split them up into three different sections.

- Core expenditures – these are expenditures that are likely to continue for the foreseeable future without change. So if you lose your job or are unable to work or even when you get to retirement, broadly these expenditures would stay the same. So examples here would be, food bills, the cost of the upkeep of the car, utility bills etc.

- Financial commitments – these are commitments that could be quite substantial but may well cease at some point in the future. For example a mortgage payment is likely to be a financial commitment. You will ultimately pay your mortgage off at some point in the future. You may have contributions into pension schemes or other saving pots that are likely to stop at say retirement. You may have an endowment that will stop with your mortgage. Likewise insurance premiums, a lot of insurance policies will have a set maturity date thereafter you are no longer paying the premiums. Certainly for people who are working now they will spend more than what they will in retirement on their financial commitments. We ordinarily record incomes gross (or before tax) so any tax and National Insurance which you pay should be recorded as a financial expenditure.

- Discretionary items. These are things that are again probably likely to continue for the foreseeable future, but if push came to shove you could reduce them. Here you are looking at travel, holidays and other discretionary items. These are important, you should not ignore them - these are the things that make life worth living.

The Budget Extender

	Current Position		
	Self	Partner	Joint
	£ 2,523	£ 1,390	£ 0
Income:			
Basic Earned Income	£	£	£
Additional Earned Income (bonus, overtime etc.)	£	£	£
Interest	£	£	£
Dividends	£	£	£
Rental Income (net of expenses)	£	£	£
Private Pension	£		£
State Pension	£	£	
Total Gross Monthly Income:		£	

The Budget Extender tries to give you an idea of all the various different items you spend money on. Crucially you should start off this analysis as of today whilst you are still working. The starting point for any prospective budget analysis is always what you are spending your money on today.

What are the things people miss?

Everyone can put their bills and direct debits into such an analysis but what are the things they miss? One example of this is car depreciation. You will need to renew your car at some point in the future, and the cost of that car is likely to be more than what your existing car could be exchanged for, so you will need to find the difference and make an allowance for that. So for example:

Imagine you currently own a car valued at £5,000. If you were to replace that car today, you would likely spend a total of £10,000. However, it is also likely that you will actually replace the vehicle in (say) three years' time, when your current vehicle may have depreciated to £2,000 in value. At that time, the equivalent new car would still cost £10,000 (inflation adjusted), meaning you would need to find £8,000 to replace your car, rather than the £5,000 it would cost you today. This £8,000 lump sum can be incorporated into your budget planner by dividing the £8,000 by three (the number of years until you replace your vehicle) and then again by twelve to convert it into a monthly expenditure. Therefore, you would need to save £222.23 per month over three years to cover the cost of upgrading the car.

You also have to include the cost of maintaining your existing home, particularly if you own your own property. This wouldn't necessarily be home improvements but it will be the cost of maintaining the fabric and fixtures of the property. This would also include garden and grounds maintenance. You will need to make an allowance for this. This is not necessarily something you will pay every month or every year but you just know that every five years you might need to repoint the garden walls, every ten years you might need to redo the drive etc.

You will also need to make allowances for 'white goods' and what you tend to spend on such things every year in terms of replacing items like televisions, laptops, gadgets and kitchen appliances.

We work out all of our client's expenditures on a monthly basis so if you see these expenditures as an annual allowance that is fine just divide that by twelve and put it on the Budget Extender.

So you have done a budget analysis for now, the next thing to do is to estimate what you will need in retirement. So take the figures as they are now and make some changes. You can start by answering the following questions:

- When we retire will our mortgage be paid off? If so delete all the expenditures that relate to the mortgage. If you have an endowment or life cover that relates to the mortgage get rid of that too.

- Do you have children and if so will they be living at home at the point you retire? If not make adjustments or deductions for the costs that are spent looking after the children.

- Would you be looking to downsize your house in retirement? Maybe the children have flown the nest and you do not need the house as it is now. What would be the cost savings if you were to downsize – council tax, utility bills etc.?

- Do you also have savings, pension or insurance premiums all of which will stop in retirement, if so delete them.

- Do you have more than one car? Would you need more than one car in retirement? What would be the cost savings that you would be able to achieve by moving down to one car? Delete the costs relating to the car which you are going to downsize from.

Also of course you can deduct your earnings so you will need to delete this income item.

On the other hand you might need to add some more things in. By definition if you are not working you have more time to fill and you will spend money to fill that time.

For example hobbies, interests and maybe more travel, so make allowances for those. We can't stress this enough. People often cost up their prospective hobbies and interests in retirement based upon the money they spend whilst they are working and perhaps have three or four weeks holiday a year at most and a few weekends or the odd evening to divert to that interest, when actually they will have far greater opportunity to enjoy their hobbies and interests when they no longer have to go to work every day.

Effectively redo the analysis on a projection basis, what does that look like, what is your income need?

You can also do a part way analysis if you are looking at more of a phased retirement so maybe working part time. So you haven't got the full expenditure items of (say) hobbies and more travel, but you have some income that is coming in but perhaps not what you are earning now. You could therefore do three different analyses: now, phased retirement and full retirement.

One thing also to be considered is not just your income items but also lump sums for example:

- Are you going to need to find a capital lump sum to pay off your mortgage when you retire?
- Are there large home improvements you need to do, what will the cost of those be?
- Are there any other purchases or one off items you want to spend or big travel plans?
- Is there any help you want to give to your children?

These should be totalled up and noted as an addition to your regular income need.

Now you need to compare this to what you have just quoted as being your existing provisions. So when you have your retirement budget extender add on the top the defined benefit income, including State Pension that you are expecting

You may need to make an allowance for income tax upon your retirement income. This doesn't need to be that complicated as many simple tax calculation tools and apps will do the work for you. Remember that when you are retired and are not earning you will not pay any National Insurance Contributions on your pension income, unlike your salary now.

When you have deducted your projected retirement expenditures from your defined benefit income is there a shortfall? If so you are going to need to make that up from defined contribution pension or other savings. Take off your defined contributions pot the lump sums expenditure plans that you have, what is left? Is there a shortfall here?

At the end of this process you may have a shortfall in either one or both of a regular income or capital need. You therefore need to accumulate savings between now and when you retire to bridge these gaps and we will explain how to do this in the next chapter.

If however you have neither an income nor capital shortfall you may have already achieved financial independence! The next stage for you would be to take some advice to confirm that this is the case and work with your adviser to bring your retirement plan to fruition!

4. How To Reduce Your Shortfall

f what you have is less than what you are going to need then you may wish to seek to bridge the shortfall. So how do you go about doing that?

The first thing you need to do before you look at the method of saving is to quantify two things. The first would be with regard to quantifying your immediate savings needs. This is where you may have a need to access the money in the near future, so certainly within the next three years. There are two potential needs for this. The first is for contingencies, money to have available to you in an emergency. Things like cash ISAs and premium bonds are good examples of types of plans people can use for rainy days. The other would be for known future expenditures. It's important to budget for items that people consider one-off, lump-sum payments that come due when the need arises. These expenditures are often habitual in nature, and while they may not occur every year, a prudent budget plan must consider them. What you should do is add those amounts up and take that off any available disposable assets.

This money should be kept in one or more cash accounts (savings account, cash ISA, National Savings etc.) that should give you access to the money when you require it and capital security. The return which you receive on these funds is somewhat of a bonus, it is not your immediate priority.

What is left is, by definition, investment capital; money that you aren't going to need in the short-term and this is what we can look to employ towards bridging this gap. Here the return upon your capital is of the greatest importance, rather than access or capital security.

The next element is in regards to surplus income. Revert to the Budget Extender that highlights what if any surplus income you have at the end of a given month, select a proportion of that which you would feel you would be able to commit over the longer term, whilst still leaving yourself with a reasonable surplus. You could for example look at some of the expenditure items and think can we cut ack here can we make savings? Make these adjustments to the udget Extender and then recalculate what you can afford to save.

s a result at the end of this process you have either surplus income hich you can afford to put away on a monthly basis and/or a lump um available to invest as a one off or a regular contribution. This is our capacity to invest.

Lump sum investment

£5,000 from Current Account
+ £25,000 from Savings Account
+ £10,000 from Premium Bonds
- £15,000 rainy day fund
- £5,000 for our anniversary holiday

= £20,000 to invest

Monthly investment

£500 surplus income
- £200 buffer

= £300 per month to invest

Where to invest?

Here there are two areas that most people should be looking at. One is a formal pension scheme and the other is a stocks and shares ISA. With retirement planning the starting point is always, if you are employed, does your employer offer you a pension scheme? If they do the following questions are worth asking:

- Do they contribute for you on your behalf?
- Do they put more money in on your behalf if you put more money in, e.g. do they match your contributions?
- Are you putting in your maximum contribution in to get their maximum contribution?

The starting point is always to look to maximise your contributions into the scheme for that reason, so you will get more employer contributions. Also if you are able to contribute more into your employer scheme even without further contributions from your employer that may also potentially save you from paying quite so many National Insurance contributions, thereby reducing the effective cost of your contributions.

This can be done through what is known as salary sacrifice or salary exchange agreement. If your employer does not have this in place you should raise this with them. The starting point for pension contributions is to get the maximum committed through your employer pension scheme, if one is available.

If it's not available or you are already paying the maximum contribution you can look to do your own thing through for example a stakeholder pension, personal pension or a Self-Invested Personal Pension.

Here you have the scope to make contributions and to potentially maximise the tax relief you have on those. You will get tax relief on all contributions up to the greater of your taxable earned income (i.e. salary and not rental or investment income) or £3,600 p.a.

At the moment under current rules the benefit you would get from contributing into a pension scheme is dependent upon how much you earn. If you are a 40% tax payer you will get up to 40% tax relief on your contributions. If you are a basic rate tax payer you will get 20%. So some people if their earnings are just above the 40% threshold, may just want to contribute enough to bring them back down to 20%. Thereby maximising their relief. All your contributions should be given tax relief at source at the basic rate of 20%. If you are a higher or highest rate tax payer then you will need to claim the excess or the difference of 20%-25% through a tax return.

Movements are afoot however for the structure of tax relief on pension contributions to be changed which may mean that the relief you may get on contributions in the future, particularly if you are a higher rate taxpayer may be higher now than in the future. So it could be something of a "whilst stocks last" sale on making large tax efficient pension contributions for those who have the earnings and cash available to do so.

There are however two things that all people who have pension schemes or are looking to contribute to pension schemes need to bear in mind, there are limits beyond which you may incur adverse tax penalties. These limits are called the annual allowance and the lifetime allowance.

The annual allowance is the limit on the amount that can be contributed into a pension scheme by you or on your behalf in any one given tax year. The lifetime allowance is the maximum value of pension benefits that you can accrue over your lifetime.

The annual allowance at the moment is currently £40,000 per year on contributions and or benefit accrual if you have a final salary benefit scheme. People should check to make sure they are underneath this allowance. You can however carry forward from the previous three tax years any unused allowances. Once you have gone past three years any unused allowance is lost. Any excess over the allowance after carry forward is taxed at your marginal rate of income tax; in effect clawing back the tax relief on the contributions.

The other criteria to look at is the lifetime allowance, which from April 2016 will be £1,000,000. This is the maximum value of pension benefits which you can accrue without again incurring a tax charge. If you exceed this lifetime allowance any further benefits taken over £1,000,000 are liable to be taxed at 55%. Many people would not want to incur this tax charge if they could get their pension benefits above £1,000,000.

Points to note here would be you can protect your benefits if you have already got £1,000,000 in benefits but that could mean stopping your contributions now or limiting the potential for further growth. This is an area where people really need to take advice. The vast majority of pension savers are not however likely to be effected by the £1,000,000 threshold.

If you have already maximised your pension savings, or indeed your tax relief on contributions and have further funds to save then the stocks and shares ISA would likely be the next best alternative.

An ISA is very similar to a pension in that it is a tax wrapper around which an investment is held which confers certain tax benefits.

With a pension the main advantages are when you put the money in as you receive tax relief of at least 20% on contributions made. With an ISA you make the contributions out of your post tax income with no income tax relief so it's not quite as tax efficient. Whilst both plans are effectively taxed the same way when they are invested, with ISAs there is no tax payable upon withdrawals. With pensions you have to pay income tax upon the majority of your withdrawals. Crucially with ISAs there is no minimum age below which you can access your funds, thereby offering many savers quite a deal of flexibility compared to pensions which cannot in most cases be access prior to age fifty-five.

There is an ISA contribution allowance limit of £15,240 per person for the 2015/16 financial year which should not be exceeded. The ISA allowance does go up every year with inflation. The ISA allowance has gone up quite significantly over the past number of years and this an help you to build up a potentially very large savings pot, which an provide a source of tax-free income in retirement which is also ot limited by a lifetime allowance.

deally we believe that most people will benefit from having both ension and ISA savings.

he balance really depends on whether our employer will offer you benefits hrough a pension scheme, when you will eed to access the money and also what our ability to save is. The questions to ask ourself include:

- Are you being threatened by the £40,000 annual allowance? If this is the case you should look to use ISAs to mop up any extra savings.
- Are you a 40% taxpayer now? If so pensions would grow faster from the extra tax relief you receive to that if you were a 20% taxpayer.

- Will I need to access the funds before I am fifty-five? If so the ISA may be the best way. Note that this minimum age will increase in the future.

- Am I being threatened by the lifetime allowance on pension contributions? – If so divert more funds where possible into ISAs.

- What will be my likely income tax rate in retirement compared to now? If you only expect the basic state pension and have no defined benefit pension schemes you may be a non or basic (20%) taxpayer in retirement. If you can get 40% tax relief on your pension contributions now and pay 0% or 20% when you come to withdraw the funds this would be far more attractive than if you would remain a 40% taxpayer in retirement. In the latter case the ISA alternative looks stronger.

- Are my expenditures, especially core expenditures, in retirement going to be met by state pension and/or defined benefit pension income? If not, further pension contributions from which you can achieve a secure income would help you to get greater peace of mind in retirement.

So a mixture of the two is often the way forward but with either option; a money purchase pension plan or an ISA, you need to understand where to invest the money once it's inside the plan. Here it is very important to take advice; everyone is different and everyone has different issues they need to take into account when deciding to invest. In effect the two key criteria would be:

1. Your attitude towards investment risk; how comfortable are you with seeing volatility in your ISA or pension plan.

2. The timescale to investment; i.e. how long is it until I'm likely to take money out of this plan. In effect the longer you have the more risk you can afford to take.

What we do is having sat down with our clients and understood these issues is to put together a mix of assets. Some of which will help protect the nominal value of the plan, so make sure it doesn't go down in value significantly in the short-term. Here we would use cash or fixed interest investments like bonds such as Gilts or corporate bonds. We then combine them alongside real assets, assets that will keep pace with inflation over time, so are more likely to grow but are a bit more volatile. Here we would look to use stocks and shares or commercial property funds. We mix those together in a bespoke way for each individual client.

Developing an investment strategy for both new contributions and also existing plans is of key importance – it will help your fund grow in the years to come. It is therefore key to take advice to make sure what you have already meets your needs and that you maximise the value from any additional savings which you may wish to make.

5. Protecting Your Retirement Plan For Your Family

What happens if I don't make it to retirement or I'm not able to spend all my pension funds before I die?

The way death benefits from pensions vary is quite significant from plan to plan and it depends upon whether you are a current member of a scheme or one you are no longer contributing into.

So going back to defined benefit pensions, this is a pension whereby your pension is given to you in a form of a guaranteed income per year. There is often a spousal pension, a pension payable to a spouse upon death. Also if you are still a member then there may be some death in service lump-sum benefits as well. Once your pension has started there could be a guarantee of paying you the income for a certain number of years, say up to five years, even if you die during that period.

With a money purchase pension plan the whole lot is available as a lump sum which is available normally to your family, i.e. your surviving spouse and/or to your children. This is much more flexible than a defined benefit scheme. A defined benefit scheme often gives you a more secure index-linked pension, so on a pension front it is often more valuable but a money purchase pension plan is commonly more valuable from a death benefits point of view.

Pension benefits are not normally liable to Inheritance Tax (IHT) so they shouldn't form part of your estate for Inheritance Tax purposes.

nheritance Tax is payable at 40% if your estate is above the Nil Rate and (NRB) currently £325,000).

or lump-sum death benefits, e.g. from money purchase plans, if you vere to die before you are aged seventy-five then any pension enefits, normally, are paid out tax-free without any penalty from the ension provider to any nominated beneficiary. If you die post eventy-five the new rules that are coming in are set to levy tax on 1at amount depending upon the marginal rate of the beneficiary. his could be zero, 20%, 40% or could even be 45%.

o if you have death in service benefits or a money purchase pension cheme where you have that flexibility over what to do with a lump um, you've got two options:

he first is to leave that pension to someone else, effectively deferring vhat happens to the scheme. If you die before age seventy-five they vould likely take a tax-free lump sum of the whole amount at the utset. If you pass away after your seventy-fifth birthday your eneficiary could keep the funds within the pension wrapper, rawing a taxable income as and when they needed to.

This pot could be made available to say your spouse or your children but the question here is are you comfortable with this? This is because in effect you are deferring when the tax is paid. If you had lived longer then you would have taken the money out of the pension eventually so you would have paid income tax on the fund above the tax-free lump sum. If you leave it to someone else for them to benefit they would then pay the tax on the ultimate fund left to them. It depends on things like what their needs are for pension funds and any additional income etc.

We commonly suggest that people look to leave their pension benefits where possible into a Discretionary Trust. This is where they nominate a Trust to receive their pension benefits and the beneficiaries of the Trust would be their surviving spouse if any, their children and any future generations.

What this allows us to do in terms of benefits is it gives you control about where your money goes. So if you were to create a normal nomination with the pension to pay the money to your spouse, if you die your spouse would inherit the pension. But then if your spouse marries someone else then their new spouse or their children might then ultimately get your pension fund. With the use of a Trust that should not happen because you are able to say who you like to benefit both now (e.g. your spouse) and also in the future too (e.g. your children and grandchildren). Another key benefit of using a Trust is to protect the funds for future generations against various different impacts. So firstly IHT, if you die and your spouse survives you for example the funds from your pension scheme won't be part of your estate for IHT purposes. If they are paid out of the pension and taken by your spouse as a lump-sum they will however form part of their estate for IHT purposes. So when the money is left to your children potentially 40% of your pension benefits will disappear.

Leaving money to a Trust keeps your money outside of the estate of your surviving spouse and the children, whilst still affording for the funds to be made available, often in the form of interest-free loans, to the beneficiaries.

There is also protection against various social impacts. So by nominating an individual, your spouse if they survive you or your children, if one or more of those beneficiaries were to say divorce they can potentially lose part of your pension benefits to people outside of your family bloodline. Other social impacts include the bankruptcy of a beneficiary, the impact of Long-Term Care (LTC) fees and spendthrift beneficiaries. Also certain beneficiaries' may receive means tested benefits so providing them a lump sum directly from a pension plan would mean they lose their benefits. Protecting the money under Trust for them could help protect against any of these social impacts and will ultimately help the beneficiaries.

6. What You Should Do Now

Hopefully by reading this guide you have been able to develop a greater understanding of retirement and how this is shaping up for you. To check your progress how would you answer the following questions?

- Do I know what my future retirement benefits are?
- What am I going to need in retirement, both income and lump-sum?
- What if any is my shortfall against these needs?
- What can I invest now to bridge the shortfall?
- How do I go about doing this?
- If I were to die would my pension fund go not only to whom I wanted it to go to but is it protected against going to people whom I don't want to receive my pension funds?

Whilst we hope that by going through this guide that you have been able to answer many of these questions you may feel that you need a little more help. If this is the case you need to take independent advice.

Sadly finding the right adviser for you is not often a clear cut decision and there are various things that you will need to consider, firstly the difference between a financial adviser and a financial planner.

Financial advice is often based around the conversation you have with a financial adviser about products, e.g. pension plans or ISAs. All are very important but a financial planner will actually help you understand the things discussed in this guide; what you have at the moment and what you are likely to need in the future, and then how best to bridge that gap. They will have various different fees and charging structures to reflect their planning process. We feel this approach ultimately has far greater benefits than solely being concerned with products.

When seeing if working with a chosen financial planner is for you there are three things you should seek: a Good Relationship, Creativity, and Leadership.

A Good Relationship: You and your planner needn't become best friends, but you shouldn't hate spending time with the person, either. Your personalities and values should be a match – good enough that you will trust the person with your personal information. The planner should make you think, "If something goes wrong, he or she is here to help me. My spouse will be taken care of, and my kids will know how to sort things out." This is my rule of thumb for what constitutes a Good Relationship.

Creativity: You've got problems to solve, or you need paths to achieve your goals. Creativity and expertise are an integral part of

73

what makes a good planner, as opposed to the advisor who will merely offer a limited menu of product options or a paint-by-numbers, one-size-fits all plan.

Leadership: The right planner will tell you what you need to do – even if it's not what you really want to hear. He or she will listen to who you are, and will tell you how to accomplish your visions. He or she will eliminate the things you don't want, and help you accomplish things you do want.

Believe it or not, anyone can call himself or herself a financial planner in the U.K., but that doesn't make him or her an expert planner. Regardless of how many words or initials follow someone's name, the designations that truly matter are Chartered Financial Planner, which is bestowed by the Personal Finance Society and is specific to the U.K., and Certified Financial Planner, which is granted by the Chartered Institute for Securities & Investment (the U.K. administrator of the International Board of Standards and Practices for Certified Financial Planners). Financial planners who are members of these organisations must pass rigorous tests and commit to continuing professional development to retain those designations.

Whilst someone with the Chartered Financial Planner and/or Certified Financial Planner designation isn't guaranteed to be a superstar, these certifications demonstrate a certain seriousness of purpose and commitment to excellence that someone without the designations may lack. At a minimum, someone with these designations is less of an "unknown quantity" than someone who hasn't bothered to take the exams and commit to ongoing professional development.

What questions should you ask when interviewing a financial planner? Here are the most basic questions that I can recommend:

1. How do you work with your clients?
2. Do you work with a certain type of client?
3. What are your qualifications?
4. What experience do you have?
5. Can you tell me about your team?
6. How do I pay you?
7. What services do you provide, and what don't you provide?
8. What is it like to be your client?

Red Flags: If the person's process doesn't revolve around a plan (i.e., solutions instead of products), continue your search. You should also look elsewhere if the planner doesn't work with people like you – people with similar backgrounds, incomes, and asset levels – or if the planner lacks significant experience, doesn't have a support team, or has no basic qualifications. And if the person can't be specific about how he or she is paid, or is dependent on selling products to generate income, you should run from the office instead of merely walking.

Green Flags: Good responses to the questions above include specific and documented approaches to the planning process; someone who works only (or predominantly) with a certain type of client – a client like you – and who has experience in working with this type of client. The planner should also have a support team that includes paraplanners and other specialists, and should be a Chartered Financial Planner and/or a Certified Financial Planner. A good planner will thoroughly and transparently explain the fee structure, and should be happy to talk about what they do and what they don't do.

If you would like to find out more about our financial planning service at Ian King Financial Planning, and indeed ask us the questions we have suggested above we would be delighted to talk with you. To start the conversation please call us on 01332 856373 or email us via info@iankingfp.co.uk

www.ingramcontent.com/pod-product-compliance
Lightning Source LLC
Chambersburg PA
CBHW041716200326

41519CB00005B/268